One Master

A call to bring prayer back into American schools

Angela Yvette

WestBow
PRESS
A DIVISION OF THOMAS NELSON

Scripture quotations are from Women's Devotional Bible, NIV-Zondervan Publishing House, Copyright, 1994.

Scripture quotations also from The Prophecy Bible KJV, 2002, Morriss Cerrello World Evangelism.

WestBow Press books may be ordered through booksellers or by contacting:

WestBow Press
A Division of Thomas Nelson
1663 Liberty Drive
Bloomington, IN 47403
www.westbowpress.com
1-(866) 928-1240

ISBN: 978-1-4497-1953-1 (sc)
ISBN: 978-1-4497-1954-8 (e)

Library of Congress Control Number: 2011931042

Printed in the United States of America

WestBow Press rev. date: 6/21/2011

Dedication

To my mommy who gave me the notion to write about this necessary campaign.

Epigraph

"Your birth is evidence that your purpose is necessary". Myles Munroe

Preface

Listen to me, you islands; hear this, you distant nations: Before I was born the Lord called me; from my birth he has made mention of my name. Isaiah 49:1

Introduction

Fifty-two out of the fifty-five framers of the United States Constitution were covert and overt impassioned Christian believers in the Holy Bible. Historically speaking, and foundationally recorded, adherence to the Bible's literal and structured sentimental blueprint is enough to affirm that this country was and is one nation founded under God. Our forefathers acknowledge God the creator of heaven and earth, in their private prayer time, and their public documents and admonishments.

From our first president George Washington to present-day leaders, this nation was birthed and led by a group of selected, saved, and spirited individuals who were specifically designed to catapult America to supernatural greatness. This amplitude was based on and guaranteed by their belief, thoughts, and relationship with our divine creator.

Our founding fathers had great fervor and passion for God and country. They were spiritual soldiers who were dedicated to a Holy God and a newly formed America. The kinship they experienced with God influenced their actions and deportment. For all intents and purposes, these thoughts dictated how they shaped and governed our country. Their relationship to God and with Him was a conduit to His kingdom, not a religion.

Proverbs 23:7 reads, "As a man thinks, so is he." What man holds in his heart or thinks in his mind greatly influences him spiritually, socially, mentally, and physically. Thoughts impact our decisions, choices, and how we operate in daily life. Our ideas inform our lifestyle, what we choose to eat, where we choose to live, worship, shop, and attend school or work.

The framework of this nation is based on a belief in a Sovereign God. Thusly, our government, law, military, insurance, housing, education, retail, food, energy, and other industries are also inspired by the original desires and intentions of our founding architects who believed in a Sovereign God.

The founding architects of this nation had a natural spiritual relationship with God. They daily determined to maintain and nurture that relationship. Theirs was a personal relationship, not a political agenda. They believed in moral and theological principles where there was no compromise. Throughout this undertaking, I will include writings as support for our leaders' ardent adherence to the word.

Anytime the originals referenced and gave honor to God, Creator, The Lord or any other biblical divine address in our original documents, the sentiment was dedicated to the God of the Holy Bible. Our founding architects sought God for direction, protection, and wisdom as to the governing order of this great nation. Whether in military, economics, family, or education, our government looked to God for guidance.

This manifest dedication was based on trust and assurance guarded by a conviction to be benevolent, unwavering, and matchless in their agenda to be a liberated and regal super power of the world. Their faith in a divine purpose was steadfast and unmovable. They knew that all things were possible with God.

Firstly, George Washington a man of faith who was fervent in his role as president and military leader of this great nation, signed the Constitution for the United States, "in the year of our Lord, 1787." To those who say that there is no mention of God or Jesus Christ in the Constitution, I ask the question: Which "Lord" was Washington referring to? King George, Lord of England? Or was it the Lord Jesus Christ, who was born 1,787 years previously and whose birth became the point of reference for all Western calendars?"

Here, one of our founding fathers advocated a life to be lived through the lens and direction of Jesus Christ. Washington fondly and earnestly spoke of his Christian faith, spreading the gospel, and Christianizing this country.

As a man thinks so is he. The founding fathers thought God, they proclaimed God, and they lived God. They voluntarily and naturally welcomed His precepts as the guide of their daily operations. Their thoughts and writings were spontaneously, intentionally, and naturally laden with biblical spiritual reference and revelation. These visions supernaturally granted them motivation and privilege to fashion our American landscape as a biblical and spiritual giant on this earth; for a reason and in this specific season.

America was ordained to be a catalyst for Christ like change here on the earth. We were created and destined to proclaim the good news of the Kingdom of God and occupy the earth until our Savior's sure return. Maranatha, the King is coming.

The Kingdom of God is love, joy, peace, and righteousness. Our founding fathers, believed in life, liberty, and the pursuit of happiness. As a standard, they used the Holy Bible as spiritual document of choice, as it traversed the tranquil oceans to this fertile land by the first aboriginal and

English settlers. As the pilgrims fled persecution, they determined to set a new course for the rest of the unchartered world to become aware of the good news of the Kingdom.

Those pilgrims who traveled to America had a divine desire of advancing the gospel of the Kingdom of Christ to distant parts of the world; this decision prompted them to leave England. The first 120 pilgrims lived by the mandate, The great hope, for the propagating and advancing the gospel of the kingdom of Christ in those remote parts of the world.

In the beginnings of the "New World" the emphasis was on fulfilling the great commission as commanded and urged by Jesus to his disciples and those to follow. In Matthew 28, 18 and 20, these are the words of Jesus, "All authority in heaven and on earth has been given to me. Therefore go and make disciples of all nations, baptizing them in the name of the Father and of the Son and of the Holy Spirit, and teaching them to obey everything I have commanded you. And surely I am with you always to the very end of the age."

What parallels and how appropriate the poetic and patriotic posture of praise and planning for a spiritual charge and mandate in "Kingdomizing" the world for Christ. The hope was to be a beacon of light, a solid spiritual promise, a city that is set on a hill. The plan sounded promising and eventually prevailed. After settling and setting up a government, our founding fathers were prepared to construct and shape a country for all people to experience the promises of joy, love, and eternal life through Jesus, as promised in the Holy Bible.

Their fervency has become infectious. According to Matthew 13: 31 - 32,

"The Kingdom of heaven is like a mustard seed, which a man took and planted in his field. Though it is the smallest of all your seeds, yet when it grows, it is the largest of garden plants and becomes a tree, so that the birds of the air come and perch on its branches."

May God, through me, let the influence pervade. I am excited to boldly share and convey these confidences based on interpretation from research, records, and other observations that I have made as a citizen of America, but more accurately a citizen of heaven.

People long for and need heavenly citizenship through Christ; Every human is searching for a relationship with the King of kings. This birthright is not based on ethnic, social, financial, or familial background. One receives the entitlement through confession of the one and only true God, and our founders recognized this kingdom commitment.

Scripture which embraces the aforementioned tradition is found in 2 Corinthians 3:17. It reads, "Now the Lord is the Spirit, and where the Spirit of the Lord is, there is liberty." We are all free in Christ. No man made law can dictate or negate God's ultimate plan for his people. He planned redemption for all who believe.

Philippians 2 verse 10 reads, "That at the name of Jesus every knee should bow, in heaven and on earth and under earth." Every knee includes, brown, black, white, olive, yellow, red, all men shall bow to the truths and tenets of our Lord and his Christ.

The Kingdom of God can be experienced by anyone, but there are prerequisites. One must follow the precepts as proposed in the covenant, the Holy Bible. The first historical framers' scriptural thoughts and ideals informed how they framed our original documents, such as the Constitution, Bill of Rights, other ordinances, and how our national holidays were celebrated, amid a plethora of other structured ceremonies practiced within our nation. Whether or not we desire to embrace or express it, "This is One Nation Under God," A nation in which God has, since our country's inception, informed our government, education, economy, law, insurance, family, and other facets of American life.

With this knowledge of scripture and divinity deeply rooted in America's genesis, I pondered why a struggle to maintain and promote our spiritual sanity and free expression of hope through Christ has become such an allergy to America.

Although I understand that we are in a culture war, our leanings and faith in Christ are what have made this country so great, prosperous, revered, and ultimately hated by others. In John 15: 18 - 19, Jesus said, "If the world hates you, keep in mind that it hated me first. If you belonged to the world, it would love you as its own. As it is, you do not belong to the world. That is why the world hates you." Even though we are hated as believers, we must be of good cheer for we are not of this world. We have a mission to complete before Christ's return.

So why have we lapsed in our judgment and living in righteousness?

Why are simple, natural, necessary, and loving behaviors such a mode of discontentment for the masses? Things such as kindness to our fellow man, hope for our future, and concern for others have become a figment or a startle to our imagination.

In present America, one could be hard pressed to find a person relating a kind word or gesture without the promise of presents or reward. A genuine gesture of love has somehow been lost in the lackluster show of life.

Without question, God is love. For God so loved the world that he gave his only begotten Son, that whosoever believes in him shall not perish but have everlasting life. (John 3: 16). God is love.

So why is America in such turmoil, distress, and emotional exile from the truths that we once held so dear?

In this manuscript, these questions and quandaries I boldly and courageously present the following points to ponder and campaigns to crusade in hopes of sparking a fire of encouragement and a design to discuss what we as Americans need to review and then ultimately repent from for "The Kingdom of God is here" (Matthew 12:28 and Revelation 12:10).

Firstly, why is it that since I desire that my children have constant and continually biblical education in school, that I am required to pay tuition in order for my twin boys to receive said education? My objective is for them to receive a Christ-centered education, say prayer and read bible scriptures, attend chapel, and learn other structured, sound Biblical curriculum in a school that clearly is located in "One Nation under God," so why should I be required to pay to pray in a country founded under the dictates of God?

As an American in a country based on Christ, said education should be free and natural.

I want them to receive, in school, what they experience at home-- the love of Christ, God, and family-- all while proclaiming that this is one nation under God without reservation or fear of repercussion. Furthermore, why have we as a nation, suffered unprecedented violent youth crime in our nation? Why have more teen pregnancies occurred now then when I was a youth? Why is it that the divorce rate is almost fifty percent? Why is it that youth and adult suicide rates have skyrocketed? Why is it that in the 1960s, because of the rebellious and hedonistic wiles of a Baltimore mother and her son and ten parents in New York, Holy Bible believers were forced to silence the voice of one crying in the wilderness? The collective group started a cantankerous ruse that led to what we experience today as secretive and quiet or non-existent prayer or worship in schools and homes across our nation, which was built and founded upon the rock that is Christ.

These deceptive and duplicitous acts of a small group of people are disturbing, idiotic, and out of order. Wake up America.

We were designed to be a nation preparing the way, not one pandering to and placating pseudo- deities of the heathen. We were designed and commanded by our creator to be bold and courageous.

Joshua 1: 9 reads, "Have I not commanded you? Be strong and courageous. Do not be terrified; do not discouraged, for the Lord your God will be with you wherever you go."

This is the passion and purpose that lives in me and it is this agenda that I bring to this manuscript. Wake up America.

Abandon that slumbering spirit, and let's honor God and our founding fathers by freely praying in all American schools again.

And rend your heart, and not your garments, and turn unto the Lord your God, for his is gracious and compassionate, slow to anger, and abounding in love, and he relents from sending calamity.

Joel 2:13

Chapter 1

Government Documents Support God

There are many examples of the influence of Jesus Christ and Christianity in America's foundational records, preserved in the annals of the Library of Congress. The Continental Confederation of Congress, a legislative body that governed the United States from 1774-1789, promoted a nondenominational Christianity.

The Second Continental Congress set aside a day specifically for prayer and purgation. Chaplains were judiciously appointed by our leaders, and all of them sponsored the publication of the Holy Bible. There was a National Humiliation, Fasting, and Prayer Day that commenced in 1776, a portion of the 1776 National Day of Humiliation, Fasting, and Prayer reads as follows:

> "In times of impending calamity and distress; when the liberties of America are imminently endangered by the secret machinations and open assaults of an insidious and vindictive administration, it becomes the indispensable duty of these hitherto free and happy colonies, with

true penitence of heart, and the most reverent devotion,
publically to acknowledge the over ruling providence of
God; to confess and deplore our offences against him."

Succinctly put, when America faced challenges, we were historically and spiritually mandated and advised to repent and turn to God. Our government realized that the only way to experience cleansing, protection, and grace from God, was to humble ourselves and repent.

The 1776 document further goes on to read, "That we may with united hearts, confess and bewail our manifold sins and transgressions, and by sincere repentance and amendment of life, appease his righteous displeasure, and through the merits and mediation of Jesus Christ, obtain his pardon and forgiveness; humbly imploring his assistance to frustrate the cruel purposes of our unnatural enemies; and by inclining their hearts to justice and benevolence, prevent the further effusion of kindred blood."

In addition to the aforementioned and set aside day of repentance, America openly prayed to God for the power and wisdom of how to defeat our enemies. The prayer further includes protection for representatives of Congress and for God to grant them the wisdom to choose the most appropriate path for America. Again, this was and is, One Nation under God. As true yesterday as is today, we must pray for our leaders.

The letter was sealed this way, "And it is recommended to Christians of all denominations, to assemble for public worship, and abstain from servile labour on said day."

A medical doctor will recommend that individuals get good rest, eat vegetables, and drink plenty of water in order to live a productive, quality life. Individuals want the good life, so they adhere to a medical doctor's provocation. Like a doctor, our founding fathers were simply beseeching America of what to do in order to live a fruitful life, and I purport that this recommendation for our country to return to God is analogous to the request of a medical professional. Said requests lead to a life filled with quality and purpose for individuals and the community. These mantras are just as necessary yesterday as there are now. Jesus Christ the same yesterday, today, and forever.

December 18, 1777, Congress established a Congressional Thanksgiving Day Proclamation which read, "American people may express the grateful feelings of their hearts and consecrate themselves to the service of their divine benefactor and join the penitent confession of their manifold sins that may please God, through their merits of Jesus Christ" (Library of Congress, 1777). The people were thankful to God for a good harvest, safe voyage, family, and peace. Additionally, the citizenry was grateful to have been given a bountiful and prosperous harvest. Our founding architects based sowing and reaping on strict adherence to their faith in God and as evidenced in the dictates presented in the Holy Bible.

Additionally, on this first National Day of Thanksgiving, under our United States' Constitution, George Washington stated, "It is the duty of all Nations to acknowledge the providence of Almighty God, to obey his will, to be grateful for his benefits, and humbly to implore his protection and favor."

Furthermore, the motto, "In God We Trust" appeared on United States coins in 1864 because of the increased religious sentiment that existed during the Civil War, and since 1938 all coins have borne said motto. On July 11, 1955 "In God We Trust" became required language on all coins and currency by an Act of Congress, and the motto was progressively added to paper money over a period from 1957 to 1966. In the United States Court of Appeals for the Ninth Circuit the ruling was as follows:

"It is quite obvious that the national motto and the slogan on coinage and currency 'In God We Trust' had nothing whatsoever to do with the establishment of religion. Its use is of patriotic or ceremonial character and bears no true resemblance to a governmental sponsorship of a religious exercise." Keep in mind that relationship has to do with intimacy. It involves a heart that is in support of and in reverential fear and love of a person, place, or thing. Religion embodies a set of rules, tenets, and ways of doing things in an orderly fashion in hopes of ensuring a productive citizenry.

I have determined that the decision to include God on our money was concretely based on natural and relational experience and respect to the creator of heaven and earth, God the Father, Son, and Holy Ghost. Whether overt or covert, the jurisprudence decision was about relationship; an authentic, natural, and supernatural relationship shared amongst believers. These believers were loyal yoke fellows in American government and law. The desire to include God in every aspect of American history was admirable and necessary.

I opine that the sentiment still exists in the hearts of Christians in America today. According to a Gallup Poll, 90% of Americans approve of the "In God We Trust" motto on U.S. currency. Let us welcome that spirit again here in America.

Through the urging of many devout American Christian leaders and dedicated politicians such as: George Washington, Benjamin Franklin, Thomas Jefferson, Patrick Henry, Andrew Johnson, Secretary of Treasury Salmon P. Chase, Chief Justice John Marshall, John Hancock, Daniel Webster, and Charles Thomas, a movement to reverence, honor, and proclaim a belief based on the principles taught and lived by Jesus Christ was established.

With America's harmonious pattern of manifest expression of God-fearing and relational sentiment with his son Jesus, as exhibited in our documents, historical and present-day functions, like praying before we partake in a meal, placing our right hand on the Bible in court, praying before a sporting event, and praying before the start of a school day, where has the zeal gone? Have we suddenly erred and denied our youth an opportunity to openly practice their faith and to pray in schools? How is it that a great portion of the United States has somehow become allergic to God?

Have we forgotten he is our healer? God is America's remedy to a fallen spiritual society. Since America's inception, God has been our refuge from enemies near and far. Wake up America.

When the founding fathers spoke of freedom of religion, it was not freedom from religion. According to an article, *Myths of Separation of Church and State (2004)*, "The founding fathers were God-fearing men who understood that for a country to stand, then it must have a solid foundation; the Bible was the source of this foundation. They believed that God's ways were much higher than man's ways and held firmly to the Bible as the absolute standard of truth and used the Bible as a source to form our government" (Butler, 2004).

Our education system is an integral part of our government and our culture. Thusly education, based on Christian traditions, should have, at its center, holy biblical principles. We should, again, practice our motto, In God We Trust.

Ninety-four percent of all quotes by the founding fathers came from the Bible. As a man thinks, so is he. Historically and governmentally, the Holy Bible is the influence of America's foundation. This Christian manual has guided our government, economy, and education. Therefore, to eliminate or silence its practice, influence, and impact would be egregious and adulterous. Have we left our first love?

Although there has been much hypocrisy amid America's attempt to stay rooted and grounded in its biblical traditions, ultimately the principles of good must prevail over evil. One must be mindful, nevertheless of the obvious and beneficial (America, is the World's Superpower, perhaps for only a few years more) impact of living in a society that embraces and acknowledges Kingdom of God principles as it foundation. Conversely, America is becoming a watered down, polluted, weak version of what the world once recognized. Again, were did we go wrong?

According to Pastor John Hagee, the moral state of a community is directly impacted by the religion and spirituality of a country. With reference to an attack on American education in *Day of Deception,* he writes,

"There is a strange irony here. Former communist leaders are now coming to America and inviting Christians to go to the Soviet Union to put together Christian education blocks because they're trying to repair the massive moral damage brought about by atheism. Meanwhile the Supreme Court of the United States and the ACLU are insisting that a new generation of young Americans must now try what has already failed in the former Soviet Union." (1997) Talk about a political paradox.

Hagee further goes on to convey how education has thrown the Ten Commandments out and put condoms in, or how a teacher cannot give aspirin if a student has a headache, without the permission of a parent, but can freely tell a pregnant student about abortion and even provide transportation to a clinic. Oh, how America has been spiritually and morally deceived!

Hagee along with many other Americans vehemently believe that in order to separate truth from falsehood, we must put God first, via Christian spirituality, and invite him back into our government, school, family, media, and all facets of American life. We are sorry God.

A piece of literature surfaced in the 1990s titled, "What Happens When You Take God Out of Schools", and it reads,

> "In light of the recent shooting in Massachusetts, let's see, I think it started when Madeline Murray O'Hare complained she didn't want any prayer in our schools, and we said OK.

> Then someone said you better not read the Bible in school…the Bible that says thou shall not kill, thou shall not steal, and love your neighbor as yourself. And we said OK.

> Dr. Benjamin Shock said we shouldn't spank our children when they misbehave because their little personalities would be warped and we might damage their self-esteem. And we said, an expert should know what he's talking about so we said OK, we won't spank them anymore.

> Then someone said teachers and principals better not discipline our children when they misbehave. And the school administrators said no faculty member in this school better touch a student when they misbehave because we don't want any bad publicity, and we surely don't want to be sued. (There's a big difference between disciplining and

touching, beating, smacking, humiliating, kicking, etc.) And we accepted their reasoning.

Then someone said, let's let our daughters have abortions if they want, and they won't even have to tell their parents. And we said, that's a grand idea.

Then some wise school board member said, since boys will be boys and they're going to do it anyway, let's give our sons all the condoms they want, so they can have all the fun they desire, and we won't have to tell their parents they got them at school. And we said, that's another great idea.

Then some of our top elected officials said it doesn't matter what we do in private as long as we do our jobs. And we agreeing with them, we said it doesn't matter to me what anyone, including the President, does in private as long as I have a job and the economy is good.

And then someone said let's print magazines with pictures of nude women (and nude men) and call it wholesome, down-to-earth appreciation for the beauty of the female and male body. And we said we have no problem with that.

And someone else took that appreciation a step further and published pictures of nude children and then stepped further still by making them available on the internet. And we said they're entitled to their free speech.

And the entertainment industry said let's make TV shows and movies that promote profanity, violence, and illicit sex.

And let's record music that encourages rape, drugs, murder, suicide, and satanic themes, And we said it's just entertainment, it has no adverse effect, and nobody takes it seriously anyway, so go right ahead.

Now we're asking ourselves why our children have no conscience, why they don't know right from wrong, and why it doesn't bother them to kill strangers, their classmates, and themselves.

Probably, if we think about it long and hard enough, we can figure it out. I think it has a great deal to do with "We Reap What We Sow."

Makes you think.

Americans, Holy Bible believing, faith possessing folk, what have we allowed to invade our holy ground?

Here in America, we are experiencing a culture war. There is a war of values, a war of good versus evil. Sadly, believers in Christ have allowed the enemy to malign, disengage, trick, and falsify the truth of our spiritual Christian heritage here in America. The media has popularized ideas of relativism, sexual freedom, idolatry, disrespect to authority, and disorder in the home. These alternative life choices have helped to make these ideas pervasive in our culture but repulsion to God.

"Sex sells" has become a universal marketing tool. The sexual revolution of the 1960s was a direct attack on the traditional notion of family, life, love, and happiness. The sleaze that our youth witness is lewd, salacious, and an abomination of God's divine and righteous plan of family. Our family, God's family is defined as a marriage between a man and a woman. Genesis 1: 27 states, "So God created man in his own image, in the image of God he created him; male and female he created them." Chapter 1 of Genesis concludes with a description of God blessing them and giving them dominion over the earth. Man and woman were created to rule the earth in a blessed and righteous manner. We are to occupy until the Lord returns.

We are a nation founded under the God of Abraham, Isaac, and Jacob; the God who founded Heaven and Earth; the God who sent his son Jesus to die for our sins, and who rose again, and who is to return to receive those unto himself, who believe.

One of the greatest goof ups in history has been the liberal rewriting of American history. The deed has included the attempted exile and total exclusion of our Christian heritage and biblical legacy. But to retard the founding architects as secular humanist men or deist who had little use of God or religion, or more importantly a relationship to Jesus Christ, is an abomination.

The governments of this nation have erred when they attempted to pass laws unjustly, and promote their evil agendas. Any law that is against God must be eradicated by believers. And when prayer was taken out of schools, it was unjust. To remove prayer from schools was unfair. This is a nation founded under God.

Therefore, America must cease and desist with the promotion of pluralism and get back to our theocracy of serving our one and true God. Prayer in Schools. Prayer in Homes.

Be strong and very courageous. Be careful to obey all the law my servant Moses gave you; do not turn from it to the right or to the left, that you may be successful wherever you go.

Joshua 1:7

Chapter 2

The Catholic Education System May Have It Right

My mother always raves about the fantastic, structured, faith-based, community-oriented, and valuable education that my sister and I received when we attended Catholic school. Although at the time we were parishioners of a Baptist church, the focus of experiencing prayer, referencing the Holy Bible and daily emphasis on love of fellow man, was the impetus for our matriculation into the Catholic school system. Our tenure in this education milieu was a short-lived two years, to this day mom expresses the noticeable difference between a public-secular, and a religious-based education. Oh how she desired that we could have attended Catholic school longer.

The financial responsibilities of tuition, however, became too great for my parents to afford. Therefore, we had to matriculate back into public school. My sister and I excelled academically by eventually attaining advanced degrees and becoming productive members in society. She is a successful entrepreneur with a Master's in Education, and I am an accomplished author and previous college professor, with a PhD in Educational Leadership.

The discipline and daily examples of rote memorization and foundational truths of communal, biblical, and Christ-like structure that we received in Catholic school were not evident in our public-American school system. In the public school, the guide of spiritual understanding, the foundational and all encompassing code and command of a loving and just God, was not present. Weekly we went to Mass and partook in a Catholic ritual. We also memorized life giving scriptures, and expressed manners as emulated in the Bible from Mary, Christ, and the disciples. We had many opportunities to raise money for community which helped us support the mission.

According to a 2011 article retrieved from Fox News, Catholic schools are doing more with less. Although Catholic schools spend more than $2,000 less per pupil than public schools, they record fierce and commendable academic achievement. "A 2009 comparison between public and Catholic school SAT scores show that public school students had an overall average of 496 points on the critical reading portion of the test while Catholic school students scored 533 points on the same portion. Catholic school students outscored their public school counterparts by an average of 23 points."

The success, pundits posit, could be due to discipline, parents' desire and motivation to be involved spiritually, socially and financially, and that "Catholics in the teaching field feel the spiritual tug of serving their church's mission in the classroom." Simply put, they are free to express and live out their relationship with Christ to their students without fear of punishment or eschewal from a system tricked by a taint of secularism as practiced in the public school.

Within the Catholic school system, they seek to promote human respect and dignity in the small communities allowing a dialogue of love, equality and social justice to flourish. Tenets based on the life and purpose of Christ and excellence in education. Promotion of these foundational truths in a structured format and Bible-based curriculum contribute to lifelong success for many students. Moreover, the combination of these attributes, elucidate distinctions in what is taught in religious education in comparison to secular education. Additionally, a structured Catholic school system believes in practicing respect and love for your fellow man, a responsibility that is admonished in the Holy Bible. The Catholic education system is sensitive to the familial needs as preached in the Holy Bible. For example, they promote that marriage is between one man and one woman, discipline of students, love neighbor as yourself, give of tithe, time and talent to your local parish, and respect government and country.

Catholic schools are not concerned with myriad value systems that currently pervade our American culture. Said perspectives manipulate and penetrate the public schools and add to the confusion and disarray found in the student and student life in and out of school and in the education system. In the parochial system, one experiences the converse; a lucid proliferation of biblical truth is encouraged and lovingly promoted. Christian beliefs and doctrines are what guide foundational perspectives of the Catholic faith. This proliferation of faith overflows into the school's curriculum and rules, and eventually, yet purposely spills over into the community and the home of its students. These thoughts of faith influence the students, home, and community. The family and the school work hand in hand to provide a solid home life for students. Prayerfully the cycle of love and obedience in the faith continues.

The most unforgettable memory that I have of Catholic education is being physically paddled by Sister Mary. Sister Mary was my third grade teacher and the first teacher to physically discipline me for inappropriate deportment. I received a swat with a wooden paddle. Although the experience was a major embarrassment, I really appreciated her (well, not really at that moment) and understood why she chose that method of punishment and sheer expression of love. Simply put, I deserved it. Also, I recall all the spankings that I received from my parents. As we press to reignite prayer in schools, we should also focus on reinstituting corporal punishment in the school system. The Bible admonishes parents that if you spare the rod, you spoil the child (Proverbs 13:24).

Today, I can report that I understand her strict stance. It is similar to what I experienced when I misbehaved, embarrassed my parents, and experienced physical and emotional reprimand. Sister Mary's approach was cushioned by Christian love and her faith in God. Since my loving parents believed in spankings, they agreed with Sister Mary's form of discipline wholeheartedly. My teacher believed that I was a good student and she was willing to work with me to help further my understanding of my God given capabilities, by all means necessary. She reasoned that my attempt to be a class clown was not going to get in the way of a much bigger and purposeful destiny. In gaining control of me, she was taking dominion over rebellious spirit. My aforementioned disruption would not be permitted to operate in her classroom. Sister Mary was given the natural and supernatural authority to curtail and control everyone in her class, and she did just that.

Daily, we students of the Catholic school system encountered, unity through weekly masses, bible readings, and familial requirements of parents to be involved with their child's education. These decrees were and still are valued and practiced in Catholic school systems.

When researching other information about Catholic education, I examined schools located in Oregon, Ontario, and New Jersey, and speaking from what I recall while attending Catholic school in Ohio, the objectives are universal. Catholic schools acknowledge learning as a lifelong process that collaborates with parents and embraces Christian beliefs and value systems. The academic missions are extended. According to an article posted on the internet (2004) O'Hara Catholic which is located in Oregon, "A good education maximizes a child's chances for a fulfilling life, and the most impressionable and formative years are elementary school years. In a Catholic school, Christian values are practiced and learned each and every day. Catholic schools teach to love God and neighbor without the (secular and pluralistic, my words) roadblocks found in public schools."

In a New Jersey Catholic school (2004), "the philosophy challenges students to improve the world by sharing gospel values and living Christ's message of salvation. They grow to understand the roots of their faith and their responsibilities as a Christian." In York Catholic District, which is located in Ontario, Canada, the Ministry of education sets the curriculum. Furthermore, they stress that, "we are called to serve and are accountable for maximizing student learning with Jesus as our inspiration." They believe that learning begins at birth and in the nurturing environment of the home. The acknowledgement that this district is "called" confirms that fact of the relationship of faith and realization in the power of the heart, further associating the principles of Jesus Christ is their ultimate goal in educating students. First Corinthians 7:17 reads, "Nevertheless, each one should retain the place in life that the Lord assigned to him and to which God has called him." Being called centers the existence on soul, spirit, and heart of the individual, embracing the belief in the supernatural, with Jesus as the foundation.

Additionally, these students study faith through scriptures and learn self-discipline and commitment, two characteristics that are an asset in succeeding in education and in life. They practice an adherence to the good news of the Holy Bible to lead the students into a prosperous and productive life. The standard virtue is taken seriously as a major variable for achieving academic success within this Catholic and Christian educational setting. There is a moral responsibility on the part of any school system, teachers, and parents to work together to fulfill the great commission of the kingdom.

Overall, this spiritual approach to education embraces, proclaims, and promotes the value of Christ and his principles being taught in and lived throughout school and community. Faith and morality are integral components of Catholic education, as similarly taught in Christian education.

As previously stated, my second grade twins have attended a Christ-centered school since kindergarten. When I initially walked in the school for a tour, I felt peace, love, and joy. I knew that was where I desired my children to receive their education. The mission statement reads, "Cincinnati Christian Schools (CCS) partnering with Christian families provides a bible-centered, quality educational program to equip, train, and discipline students to follow Christ and impact culture."

And since 1971, Christian business leaders and educators have assembled together to provide just that. CCS is fulfilling the great commission as conveyed by Jesus Christ and the architects of our American society. It is a privilege to be a part of the CCS community.

Christ-centered schools and the Catholic education system have witnessed significant academic and social success due to the austere adherence and practice of a faith that is founded on the life of Jesus Christ. Yes, I believe mom and dad were correct in their desire to provide us with a Christ-centered education. They realized the bountiful spiritual and natural benefit of rote memorization of the fruit of the spirit: love, joy, peace, patience, kindness, goodness, faithfulness, and self-control. Against these there is no law. (Galatians 5:22-23) My parents knew it. The founding fathers knew it. America used to know it. Wake up America. We must bring prayer to Jesus back into our public schools.

You are witnesses of these things.

Luke 24: 48

Chapter 3

The Evidence is Lucid

In 1951, the New York State Board of Regents (the state board of education) approved a 22-word "nondenominational prayer" to be recited every morning in American public schools. It read, "Almighty God, we acknowledge our dependence upon Thee, and we beg Thy blessings upon us, our parents, our teachers and our country."

This prayer, which was read aloud, permeated the academic atmosphere with words of hope and encouragement that asked God to bless our youth, family, education, and nation. The objective of the prayer was to acknowledge dependence on Almighty God and recognize the need to emphasize moral and good character through a recitation about that which the students were engaged in on a daily basis, their interactions with family, education, nation, and self.

The purpose was not to promote wicked or evil thoughts that plagued the nation. The agenda was not to promote war, promiscuity, vulgarity, divorce, or chicanery. The mission was to think of those things which are pure, holy, and lovely. Philippians 4: 8-9 reads,

"Finally, brethren, whatsoever things are true, whatsoever things are honest, whatsoever things are just, whatsoever things are pure, whatsoever things are lovely, whatsoever things are of good report; if there be any virtue, and if there be any praise, think on these things. Whatever you have learned or received or heard from me, or seen in me—put it into practice. And the God of peace will be with you."

The "things" are to be learned and practiced. Our youth learn in school. What a person thinks, learns, practices, and receives, so is he. Thinking of the aforementioned things of good report will solely support an environment of peace, joy, and love. Imagine that, a climate of whatever is true, noble, right, pure, lovely, admirable, excellent, and praiseworthy. Thinking on good things is exactly what the youth in American schools in 1951 were doing.

The opposite of what we experience in the schools of the 21st century is happening in our educational systems: a milieu of chaos, distrust, impurity, sadness, despair, drugs, immoral sexual activity, and disrespect. Reasons of this paradigm shift can be found in the acidic actions of a handful of American citizens. The conversion commenced when parents of 10 students objected to the optional, morning prayer. Here, ten bad apples spoiled a whole precious program. The prayer was voluntary. If the parents or students refused to recite said prayer, all they were required to do was bring in a note of declination.

Instead, this group decided to fight the powers that be. The cacophony of darkness began to silence the voice of the one crying in the wilderness, Prepare ye the way of the Lord. Sound the alarm America. The Holy One of Israel is waiting.

Instead, Satan began to go around seeking whom he may devour. First Peter 5 verse 8 reads, "Be sober, be vigilant; because your adversary the devil, as a roaring lion, walketh about, seeking whom he may devour."

And he used the parents of the ten to do his bidding.

In the subsequent court case, Engel v. Vitale (1962) the following were questions posed:

1. Did the Regents of New York violate the religious freedom by providing time during the school day for this particular prayer?

My answer: If one refused, then all they had to do was to provide a note of declination.

2. Did the prayer itself represent an unconstitutional action--in effect, the establishment of a religious code by a public agency?

My answer: Constitution is based on relationship with Lord God Almighty, not on just a miniscule tradition or words.

3. Did the Establishment Clause of the 1st Amendment prevent schools from engaging in religious "wall of separation" between church and state breached in this case?

My answer: The case is freedom of religion, not freedom from religion. And it just so happens that this is a country founded by believers of the Father, Son, and Holy Spirit.

So how was the case resolved?

By a vote 6-1 majority, the court found the New York Regents' prayer to be unconstitutional. Justice Hugo Black cited, "We think that by using its public school system to encourage recitation of the Regents' Prayer, the State of New York has adopted a practice wholly inconsistent with the

Establishment Clause. There can, of course, be no doubt that New York's program of daily classroom invocation of God's blessings…in the Regents' Prayer is a religious activity…"

Stop the presses. I can recall reading in American history books, accounts of historical educational documents, and watching wholesome television programs such as, *Little House on the Prairie*, that school was conducted in the church, and church was conducted in the schoolhouse. These two foundational American entities were housed in the same building. These two daily fundamental functions were allowed to coexist, or should I say the two naturally existed. No dichotomy, no separation, no distinction. There was an obvious and necessary partnership.

Here is an appropriate place to interject a reminder of sentimental and tenured tenets admonished in America: "This country is, One Nation Under God. In God we Trust. We have posted stone tablets of the Ten Commandments, and in court one must Swear to tell the whole truth so help you God, and documents such as, United States Constitution, and the Northwest Ordinance of 1787, just to name a few of the decrees that observed and honored in the daily operation of our society. There can be no equivocation that our Christian and Godly heritage is evident in our founding principles and ideas. So how is it that we, believers with power imbued from our maker, persist in allowing the ungodly heathen and principalities of darkness to push us around, shut us up, and alter our destiny? It's time to wake up America.

Psalm 33:12 reads, "Blessed is the nation whose God is the Lord, the people he chose for his inheritance." Succinctly put, and according to the Holy Bible, we are blessed as long as we have God as our Lord.

When we voluntarily or involuntarily ignore and remove God from government, economy, education, and the family, as seen in today's society, we recognize what happens when sin is a reproach of the nation. We witness usury prevalent in business, injustices reigning in law, and violence, abuse, immoral sex, and drugs ruining the lives of family members.

In iniquity, there is no discrimination as to the trespasser's age, gender, race, or other societal associations. All will be negatively impacted; none will be exempt. Reproach affects every facet of society and the most colossal damage is that the family is broken, crushed, battered, and embittered. This degeneration is then recycled into the individual whose is part of the broken family who then takes a job in government, education, law, military, retail, music, movies, and other entertainments. These hurting people hurt people and the brokenness continues to recycle and sin persists. The blessings dissipate and, believe it or not, the believers are the ones to blame.

Second Chronicles 7: 14 reads, "if my people, who are called by my name, will humble themselves and pray, seek my face, and turn from their wicked ways, then will I hear from heaven and will forgive their sin and will heal their land." When believers of the gospel of Christ return to God seeking him with our whole heart, then will he hear from heaven and heal our land of turmoil, slander, murder, unrest, idolatry, hatred, disparity, famine, and the like. When we return to God, it doesn't matter what our culture looks like on the inside or outside, we who are connected to the Kingdom of God win. It's that simple.

Yet, since we are not securing our position, reading, proclaiming, and living for Christ as he designed and purposed us to do, Satan the enemy and father of lies, cunningly continues to invade our earthily dominion with disarray, destruction, and deception.

Now back to the discussion of the establishment clause, Justice Black further stated, "The Establishment Clause thus stands as an expression of principle on the part of the Founders of our Constitution that religion is too personal, too sacred, too holy, to permit its 'unhallowed perversion' by a civil magistrate." Black neglected the notion that countless religious, more importantly relationship elements are associated with governments and officials, reflecting the religious heritage of the nation. We are one nation under God.

Did the justice not receive the memo of our myriad foundational documents which are overtly laden with religious and Christ relational obedience?

What is the definition of personal? According to Webster, it is anything relating to or affecting a particular person, and, I assert that what we believe in school, home, and our surroundings personally, greatly affects our macro-environment; the relationships are interconnected.

Therefore, how can a principle which details beliefs, connections, thoughts, and ideas, and is natural and reflects how one was reared be kept at bay, and defined as being too personal, especially in a nation that was founded on the principles of the life and words of Jesus Christ?

That would be like saying to anyone, "Today, I need you to stop breathing. I know you are used to doing this naturally, and your entire being is supported by this act, but today don't do what comes naturally." Realistically and physically, this is not going to happen, and if it does you would die.

And, that my friend is what's happening in America today. Why? Breathing is a natural and necessary function of our lives, just as it is for every life to honoring and worshipping of God the father. Our founding fathers proclaimed their relationship with Jesus naturally and personally. America needs Christ.

Another attack of the enemy comes from the deception in the language of "wall of separation" that was embraced in 1802 by Thomas Jefferson was as figurative analogy. This line of demarcation was based on an act of freedom of religion, not freedom from religion. It was solely as a symbol. I am most certain our founding fathers had no conception of the notion of America one day being invaded by the inauthentic religions that we are contending with today. The religion honored and reserved for our land is that which was and is supreme and esteemed in America, the one and only true philosophy and belief of acknowledging the Lord of Jesus Christ and having a relationship with him as Holy and sovereign. Simply put, the founding government officials did not have to establish a religion that was already naturally and spiritually the standard of this land.

Make no mistake people. America was founded on biblical, holy principles as inspired by the gospel according the God the Father, his son Jesus Christ, and the Holy Spirit. Our immutable rights are privileges and benefits granted and guaranteed by our God, the God of this nation.

Therefore, humble servants, the establishment of religion clause and the wall of separation mean at least the following:

> Neither a state nor the federal government may set up a church. Neither can pass laws that aid one religion, aid all religions, or prefer one religion over another. Neither can force a person to go to or remain away from church, against his will or force him to profess a belief or disbelief in any religion. Neither a state or the federal government may, openly or secretly, participate in the affairs of any religious organizations or groups and vice versa.

In the words of Jefferson, the clause against the establishment of religion by law was intended to erect a wall of separation between church and state. No interference needed. They already knew who the God of this land was; their thinking came with meditation on the bible. This law was natural, it was evident, and it was historical.

The wall was exclusively figurative and one that was and is realistically inapplicable. Why? The denominations of the framers, aboriginals, founding fathers, and leaders of America included Presbyterians, Anglicans, Puritans, Protestant, Congregationalist, Quakers, Catholic, Christians, and Calvinist. This colossal group of religious congregants was united under a common faith, a single administrative and legal hierarchy, Jesus Christ. Therefore, our nation's letters, diaries, personal writings, and legal, binding documents were framed by good Christian morals and faith guides. As a man thinks, so is he. We are one nation under God.

Yet the blurred vision and contextual liberal wall of separation continues to this day because of self-idealization, idolatry, rebellion, confusion, and ignorance. The encounter is similar to what occurred in Genesis 3. After being told by God in Chapter 2 that they should not eat of the tree of the knowledge of good and evil, Adam and Eve decided to do things their way. They ate of the forbidden fruit.

Because of this act, the reverberations are still being felt today. They rebelled and thusly separated themselves from their Almighty creator. This myopic perspective persists in plaguing mankind today. Genesis 3: 4-7 reads,

> "You will not surely die," the serpent said to the woman. For God knows that when you eat of it your eyes will be opened, and you will be like God, knowing good and evil." When the woman saw that the fruit of the tree was good for food and pleasing to the eye, and also desirable for gaining wisdom, she took some and ate it. She also

gave some to her husband, who was with her, and he ate it. Then the eyes of both of them were opened, and they realized they were naked; so they sewed fig leaves together and made coverings for themselves."

As evidenced in biblical accounts, dancing with the devil will always get one into trouble. The serpent won the encounter with mankind. Their reality was confused. Satan had deceived them, and because of this manipulation, Adam and Eve had forfeited their kingdom privilege and rightful place on this earth.

This distortion of knowledge led them to believe that they knew more than they actually did; thus, they experienced things not purposed for them such as hard labor, perpetual suffering, the first murder known to mankind, and other subsequent challenges and habitual sin that we experience and must endure in the 21st century.

Our dichotomies of religious versus secular, righteousness versus sin, peace versus unrest, prosperity versus poverty, and light versus darkness, have continued to interrupt God's original intent. But Proverbs 19:21 declares, "Many are the plans in a man's heart, but it is the Lord's purpose that prevails."

Jefferson's and others' intent of wall of separation of church and state pales in comparison to God's intent for a nation whose God is the Lord. America has proclaimed Christ as Lord, and we must resume the posture of praise to our Deliverer.

I once heard a profound statement, "the only reason why there is darkness is because of the absence of light." Believers are the light. In Matthew 5:14- 16, Jesus proclaims, "You are the light of the world. A city on a hill cannot be hidden. Neither do people light a lamp and put it under a bowl. Instead they put it on its stand, and it gives light to everyone in the house. In the same way, let your light shine before men, that they may see your good deeds and praise your Father in heaven."

Turn on the light. We are the light. America must heed this clarion call, the voice of the one crying to a dark world, serve Christ and be free. Bring prayer back in our schools.

Angela Yvette

For God so loved the world that he gave his one and only son, that whoever believes in him shall not perish but have eternal life.

John 3:16

Hear the cry of our children

Dear God,

Why didn't you save the little girl?

Sincerely,

Concerned Student

AND THE REPLY

Dear Concerned Student,

I am not allowed in schools.

Sincerely,

God

Chapter 4

Screaming for a Solution

The United States of America is in pandemonium. From an emotional, spiritual, financial, familial, and psychological perspective, America is in a distressed situation of incomprehensible proportion. The following statistics gathered from various agencies such as: National Center on Health Statistics, Department of Health and Human Services, National Youth Violence Prevention Resource Center, and Americans for Divorce Reform, demonstrate the grave state of affairs in our culture. The information highlights data retrieved from across the country and elucidate how desperate the state of affairs is here in America. Unfortunately, few efforts and little dialogue have taken place in our homes, schools, churches, or communities in order to clarify and then hopefully eradicate America of the nihilistic neighborhoods in which we find ourselves living. The problem confronts everyone; no one is exempt.

TEEN PREGNANCY

The United States has the highest rate of teen pregnancy in the Western Industrialized World.

Every year around 750,000 teens will get pregnant. The rate of teen pregnancy is highest in Nevada with 113 per 1,000 and in North Dakota it is the lowest at 42 per 1,000.

More than 2/3 of all teenagers who have a baby will not graduate from high school.

ALCOHOL and DRUGS

Underage drinking costs the US more than 58 billion every year.

Forty percent of those who started drinking at age 13 or younger developed alcohol dependence.

Teens who drink are 50 times more likely to use cocaine than teens who never use alcohol.

Twenty percent of 8th graders report they have tried marijuana.

More than sixty percent of teens said that drugs were sold, used, or kept at their school.

TEEN VIOLENT CRIME

Homicide is the second leading cause of death of young people ages 10-24.

The third leading cause of death among teens is suicide.

One of the country's deadliest school shootings occurred at Columbine High School, where two student gunmen killed 12 fellow students, one teacher, and then turned the gun on themselves.

DIVORCE

Fifty percent of marriages in America end in divorce.

Divorced women with children are four times more likely than married women to have an income that is under the poverty line.

Although ten percent of families in the U.S. are headed by a woman, forty percent of poor families have a female head of household.

Teen girls from single parent homes are twice as likely to drop out of high school and give birth to an out of wedlock child.

These abbreviated statistics show the ever increasing problems and challenges mounting in a society that has dismissed God from the very essence of its foundation. Teen pregnancy, drugs, crime, and divorce are consequences of sin. Simply put, sin is a reproach to any nation.

Because of the aforementioned aberrations, we are witnessing increasing idolatry, bearing false witness, self-centeredness, adultery, theft, practicing of magical arts, and murder. These works are diametrically opposed to what God commanded in the Ten Commandments.

Here's a reminder of the list of the ten rules that we have conveniently, arbitrarily, and ignorantly allowed to be removed from our court houses across the nation. Found in Exodus 20, we find the Ten Commandments. This list is taken from an assignment for my twins to remember and recite at the Christian School they attend.

1. Thou shall have no other gods before me.

2. Thou shall not make unto thee any graven images.

3. Thou shall not take the name of the Lord thy God in vain.

4. Remember the Sabbath day, to keep it holy.

5. Honor thy father and thy mother.

6. Thou shall not kill.

7. Thou shall not commit adultery.

8. Thou shall not steal.

9. Thou shall not bear false witness.

10. Thou shall not covet.

> God made it clear that if we adhere to this list of laws, we would have a just, civil, and peaceful society.
>
> Consider a Congressional Record joint resolution:
>
> Whereas, the Ten Commandments appear over the bench where the United States Supreme Court Justices sit, thus showing the source from whence our laws and government power of the state are derived. Whereas, America's colonial governments adopted the Ten Commandments not as an object of worship or an icon, but as the basis for their civil and criminal law. April 3, 1644, the judicial laws of God, as they were delivered to Moses be a rule to all courts in this jurisdiction.

The Ten Commandments were the law of the land. However, the Supreme Court made an unjust law when they outlawed and amended the placement of the Ten Commandments in our court rooms, and the eradication of structured, organized, and open prayer in our schools.

And since the hegemonic powers and silent believers have rejected and rebelled against God, America is experiencing more vile, shameful, and deceitful deportment by parents, children, and appointed leaders in our western world. In a nation founded under a supernatural and sovereign God, we have allowed the schemes and wiles of the defeated foe named Satan to lead our nation astray. This is not what God ordained. Read the words from Deuteronomy Chapter 6: 1-12.

These are the commands, decrees and laws the Lord your God directed me to teach you to observe in the land that you are crossing the Jordan to possess, so that you, your children and their and their children after them may fear the Lord your God as long as you live keeping all his decrees and commands that I give you, and so that you may enjoy long life. Hear, O Israel, and be careful to obey so that it may go well with you and that you may increase greatly in a land flowing with milk and honey, just as the Lord, the God of your fathers, promised you.

Hear, O Israel: The Lord our God, the Lord is one. Love the Lord your God with all your heart and with all your soul and with all your strength. These commandments that I give you today are to be upon your hearts. Impress them on your children. Talk about them when you sit at home and when you walk along the road, when you lie down and when you get up. Tie them as symbols on your hands and bind them on your foreheads. Write them on the doorframes of your houses and on your gates.

When the Lord your God brings you into the land he swore to your fathers, to Abraham, Isaac and Jacob, to give you—a land with large, flourishing cities you did not build, houses filled with all kinds of good things you did not provide, wells you did not dig, and vineyards and olive groves you did not plant—then when you eat and are satisfied, be careful that you do not forget the Lord, who brought you out of Egypt, out of the land of slavery."

The God of this nation, set commands and edicts in place that our progenitors and leaders of this nation vowed to uphold and teach to their children. These specific and lucid laws were to be taught and tied as symbols on our hearts, doorposts, and houses; the foundations were guaranteed to be unshakable.

Our God promises that when we adhere to, support, and are careful to listen to these laws, then we would experience good things such houses filled with abundance, hope, and love, liberty, life, and happiness which is endowed from our creator.

Who wouldn't serve a caring, living and true God like that? We had it all. We made the sacrifice for our children, our land, and our God. But it wasn't the sacrifice that God was after, it was an obedient heart, mind, and soul.

America, a nation under God, has decided to alter the agreement. The lips of praise to the Almighty have become luxury lips seeking to gratify self and "keep up with the Joneses." Lips now acknowledge that one can control his or her own destiny; lips now acknowledge religions that embrace an eternity which promises seventy two virgins to those who kill in the name of a false god. Lips now acknowledge allegiance to a god with a cement pot belly. Lips which acknowledge sacredness of a cow over the sacredness of the living lamb of God who gave his life for our ransom; These lips have the audacity to acknowledge that the world will end in 2012, when only the maker of heaven or earth determines when the new heaven and new earth will descend. These lips that have the nerve to suggest that we cease and desist our acknowledgement to have, "Merry Christmas" greetings in fear that we may offend someone who doesn't serve the one who came to give us life more abundantly.

Return to our God, America. The following passages were stated by Jesus after he casts out a demon- possessed man who was blind and mute, and after he healed a man's hand that was deformed. Jesus had come to bring life, healing, and deliverance to those who would accept life, receive deliverance, and live a life of abundance through him.

Matthew 12: 25-30, Jesus states how a kingdom divided against itself operates.

> Jesus knew their thoughts and said to them, Every kingdom divided against itself will be ruined, and every city or household divided against itself will not stand. If Satan drives out Satan, he is divided against himself. How then can his kingdom stand? And if I drive out demons by Beelzebub, by whom do your people drive them out? So then, they will be your judges. But if I drive out demons by the Spirit of God, then the kingdom of God has come upon you. Or again, how can anyone enter a strong man's house and carry off his possessions unless he first ties up the strong man? Then he can rob his house. He who is not with me is against me, and he who does not gather with me scatters.

Deuteronomy 6: 13- 15 states: "Fear the Lord your God, serve him only and take your oaths in his name. Do not follow other gods, the gods of the peoples around you; for the Lord your God, who is among you, is a jealous God and his anger will burn against you, and he will destroy you from the face of the land." America, we must heed the call of our God, or else. Rebellion is defined as open and organized resistance to one's government; or defiance of any authority, control, or tradition. We have rebelled against the beliefs, government, history, and spiritual dictates of this land as practiced by our founding fathers. One nation under God, the God of Abraham, Isaac and, Jacob.

Leaders and believers in this nation have allowed our spiritual and natural borders to be attacked and marauded by the ruthless and diabolic claims of false religions and deadly deeds. Secular humanism, Islam,

Hindu, Buddhism, and other inanimate and fake beliefs have illegally infiltrated our borders.

We must take back what the enemy has stolen and return to the plan of our founding fathers and our founding creator, God, Son, and Holy Spirit. We must return justice to the land.

Our God is loving, but there are prerequisites. He will hear our call if we return. But America, a nation founded under God must do what is written in 2 Chronicles 7: 14- 15, "if my people, who are called by my name, will humble themselves and pray and seek my face and turn from their wicked ways, then will I hear from heaven and will forgive their sin and heal their land. Now my eyes will be open and my ears attentive to the prayers offered in this place."

If America desires to see the teen pregnancy rate dissipate, use of alcohol and drug amongst our teens and adults to be eradicated, a decrease in violent teen crime, and the decimation of divorce amid our families, we must turn back to God.

This is our prayer for the nation, prayer in schools and prayer in families. This is our battle cry.

You must obey my laws and be careful to follow my decrees. I am the Lord your God. Keep my decrees and laws, for the man who obeys them will live by them. I am the Lord.

Leviticus 18: 4, 5

Chapter 5

Love Is The Greatest of These

The proverbs of Solomon son of David, king of Israel:

for attaining wisdom and discipline; for understanding words of insight; for acquiring a disciplined and prudent life, doing what is right and just and fair; for giving prudence to the simple, knowledge and discretion to the young—let the wise listen and add to their learning, and let the discerning get guidance—for understanding proverbs and parables, the sayings and riddles of the wise. The fear of the Lord is the beginning of knowledge, but fools despise wisdom and discipline.

The above passage of scripture, Proverbs 1:1-7, describes the benefits of wisdom. Accordingly, one could deduce that a person who acquires wisdom should experience a life of goodness, mercy, and joy. Sure, there will be times of travail and tumult, but ultimately, if one listens to knowledge, insight, and guidance of Christ, even through the pain, he or she is guaranteed comfort. This truth is promised to those who fear the Lord.

Trust is based on a pattern and willingness to follow a time tested and proven journey. Faith is conducive to believing in what is and what is to come. America has experienced a history based on devotion to the belief on God as our refuge and deliverer as related to the foundational experience, spiritual dependence, and natural relationship. Our founding fathers did not simply hold firm their conviction based on a particular religion or denomination. It was contingent upon a proven relationship with Christ.

Yes, myriad denominations are chronicled in the annals of America's history, yet the denominations are all represented by a righteousness and relationship that comes through faith and adherence to one true god, the trinity: God the Father, Son, and the Holy Spirit.

This faith in Christ is what has historically propelled the United States to great stature in the world. It is the faith that we must revert to in order to experience the prosperity, joy, peace, and abundant life that sustained us and that we once practiced.

As a believer in Christ, I am thoroughly connected to my faith and relationship with God. I practice daily devotions of reading scripture, prayer, and meditation on God. Additionally, the custom to love God and neighbor as myself, have become my daily mantra. In Matthew 22: 37-40, Jesus gives the greatest commandment. He states, "Love the Lord your God with all your heart and with all your soul and with all your mind. This is the first and greatest commandment. And the second is like it: Love your neighbor as yourself. All the law and the Prophets hang on these two commandments."

In the Old Testament, we are given the Ten Commandments in order to achieve a life of goodness which is contingent on adherence to obedience to these ten rules. Then in the New Testament, Jesus sums the laws up in two commandments. It is this fulfillment to the two expressions of love that we can experience a life and society blessed by an eternal God. Love conquers all. Our relationship to a loving God is how we accomplish life's ultimate goal. The founding fathers knew it. Believers know it. We can do it. I know we can.

This connectedness is the basis for my emphatic plea to bring back the privilege to openly pray in all schools. The benefits are obvious, impenetrable, and long-lasting.

When I matriculated into college, I roamed away from the royal mandate of Kingdom living such as reading the word and having daily prayer. Sometime thereafter, I reconnected to my redeemer and savior, Jesus Christ. Thusly, I must fulfill the great commission as commanded by the King of kings. Because of his grace I am able to testify to the wonders, signs, and miracles that have been bequeathed to me from my righteous Savior. Habakkuk 3:19 reads, "The Sovereign Lord is my strength; he makes my feet like the feet of a deer, he enables me to go on the heights." It is my recognition to God's sufficiency that I am able to ride on the heights, protection, and greatness of the Kingdom of God.

We as a nation must return to God and depend on him for all we need.

As the Bible states, "Train (start) a child in the way he should go, when he is old he will not turn from it" (Proverbs 22:6). My parents did just that, and I must say that my parents had great assistance in achieving a supernatural job.

From the aforementioned Catholic school education to the myriad church services and daily Bible readings and applications and from the finished work of Christ, I hypothesize that the angels in heaven are rejoicing. I am blessed.

My mother always taught my siblings and me that if we are studying for a test, or writing a paper, or facing any challenges in life, then we should read the book of Proverbs in order to gain a better understanding of all areas of academics and life. In so doing, we could attain the skills necessary to further our development in the learning process.

The book of Proverbs ushers in comprehension, insight, and supernatural growth. Consequently, I haven't ceased reading this wisdom. It is within these particular chapters that frustration and fear are recognized, and I am also guided how to overcome. Proverbs has been my prologue and guiding force to what is right and what is wrong.

Additionally, precepts of Proverbs have taught me how to navigate my daily decisions and activities amid life's experiences. Whether dealing with family, school, work, or other areas of life, it is through these words of wisdom that I have made it and will continue to succeed. As a man thinks, so is he. Right thinking is fundamental to right actions.

America, we must think on those things above, so we can witness the righteousness and Kingdom living that God designed from the beginning for those who will believe.

I realize that there are many religions practiced here in America, but my primary goal is to lead people to a RELATIONSHIP with Christ-- not a denomination, but a relationship.

Within everyone is a responsibility, a charge to do for self and for others. Conversely are the secular humanist movements and other pluralistic protocols practiced in America today. These campaigns promote selfishness, narcissism, and discord. I believe that individuals are not on an island existing just to please self without regard for one's fellow man.

Our charge is communal. Unfortunately, over the last century anti-God ideologies have been promoted throughout American culture. The council for Secular Humanism (2003) defines the theoretical perspective as,

> A conviction that dogmas, ideologies, and traditions whether religious, political, or social must be weighed and tested by each individual and not simply accepted on faith. A search for viable individual, social, and political principles of ethical conduct, judging them on their ability to enhance human well-being and individual responsibility without reference to religion and exclusively by means of human reason.

How can "self" determine what is beneficial for self, when self didn't make self? We must retreat and consult the manufacturer. Our creator who designed us conveyed our purpose through a manuscript called the Holy Bible. The Bible is our manual. Therefore, anything promoting and puffing up rules by dictates of self is a highly deceptive, controversial, and false worldview.

The discourse surrounding secular humanism has taken the path of where the sole focus is on the human as the god of his or her life where individual thoughts or feelings are superior to everybody and everything. Thus, human nature distorts God's way, and the truth is minimized. Oh what a tangled web we have woven!

From movies, textbooks, political and educational practices, to business and health organizations, notions that life begins with humankind and nature and not God, a sovereign deity, have coerced and silenced a once spiritually, Christ-oriented culture into a group of self-centered, egotistical, myopic and weak individuals.

Face it-- there is a logical explanation as to why our culture is witnessing more drug use, obesity, drunkenness, nihilism, self-hatred, pornography, homelessness, poverty, lewdness, and the like. The reason is rebellion from our foundation which is God. America has rebelled from the foremost desires of our founding fathers, "One Nation Under God." This anti-God state of mind has further contributed to the societal rise in violence, vulgarity, and vice. These realities have corrupted family, school, and home. However, there is hope.

I have found that we are a Christian community of individuals with varied different responsibility yet a distinct hope. This truth is evidenced in Romans 12:5-8. It reads,

> So in Christ we who are many form one body, and each member belongs to all the others. We have different gifts, according to the grace given us. If a man's gift is prophesying, let him use it in proportion to his faith. If it is serving, let him serve; if it is teaching, let him teach; if it is encouraging, let him encourage, if it is contributing to the needs of others, let him give generously; If it is leadership let him govern diligently; if it is showing mercy, let him do it cheerfully.

Life is to be lived according to the individual's faith, and that faith can help transform society into the likeness of Christ. I am persuaded that my charge in life is to teach, serve, and lead students, families, and the American community in their quest for the truth. Presently, I realize that Biblical perspectives and their application to academics can only be recognized in a private school setting. However, I believe that when the forefathers professed the separation of church and state, they had an entirely different objective in mind then what we now see being practiced in schools today. They believed in prayer in schools, government, family, military, and all other facets of American culture.

I sincerely believe that the founding architects visualized the two entities, church and state, working hand in hand. The cadence is categorically undeniable as we proceed with the discussion of a prominent piece of our history.

In 1787 the Congress of the United States passed the Northwest Ordinance which states:

"Religion, morality, and knowledge, being necessary to good government and the happiness of mankind, schools and the means of education shall forever be encouraged." Here, religion, good, and government are being used harmoniously and positively. These entities are being encouraged to co-exist.

And, according to a three-part Christian Education series presented by the Millersburg Baptist Church in Missouri, the notion of school and church coexisting as a motion is seconded. They write:

> "Nations with not only an emphasis on scripture but also a reformation base, that is they were largely protestant and stressed reading the Bible, had a literacy rate of 94-99 percent. In the 217 years from 1620 when the pilgrims landed in America to 1837 the literacy rate averaged nearly 100 percent. John Quincy Adams said in the early 19th century that only four people out of 1000 were illiterate. Today, after 150 years of public education, over 20% of Americans are either fully or functionally illiterate."

One must conclude that the heart and strength of education was and is in Christianity. In the past, the nation looked to the Bible for direction not only in a governing the nation and at a time of war, but in the teaching and learning process of the people. Moreover, the authority of the Holy Bible inspired the history of education and its pedagogy here in America, but when America abandoned this foundational truth, educational, familial, economic, and societal chaos ensued.

Let's not forget that in centuries past, the church housed and provided funding for the school. The two operated in concert. However, with the influx of heretical hoopla, and with school district lawsuits citing Christian religion, Ten Commandment, and one nation under God tenets as primary complaints to freedom of religion and as points of contention, one might conclude that America was founded with no spiritual base whatsoever. America, we have become the laughing stock of the world. We must get our house in order.

Since the debate is still in progress, I submit that my timely acumen and profound account and the historical grounding as fostered by our founding fathers of the power of knowledge via Christian spirituality and a relationship with Christ can be shared and be applicable to bringing out of the squalor that the United States finds itself.

One answer is by reinstituting prayer back in schools. It is our faith that will assist us in becoming the nation of prosperity and hope that we once were.

Faith is a ubiquitous practice in prevailing against hardships. Even our previous Christian president, George Bush (Cincinnati Enquirer, 2004) stated,

"The miracle of salvation is the key to solving some of society's most intractable problems." This profound statement was delivered at a church in New Orleans. In this church, which is in located in a crime-ridden section of the city, Bush further asserted, "Faith-based programs are only effective because they do practice faith. It's important for our government to understand that." Throughout his campaign and subsequent two terms as president of the United States, Bush was a fervent supporter of social programs, and to religious groups and the like which he believes the federal government should fund.

It is evident that from federal to state, and city to local, people are searching for answers to the baneful burdens that are afflicting the American culture. Our resolve rests in our original refuge, Jesus Christ. Put prayer back in schools.

Peace I leave with you; my peace I give you. I do not give to you as the world gives. Do not let your hearts be troubled and do not be afraid.

John 14:27

Chapter 6

I'm Not Alone

Lyrics to song, "I Refuse" by Josh Wilson, tell that someone else understands the urgent need for believers to ignite their purpose in Christ. No more empty, silent, or selfish prayers. But we need to present our earnest request to God Almighty. The chorus to the song, are as follows:

> "Sometimes I, I just want to close my eyes
> and act like everyone's alright when I know they're not.
> This world needs God, but it's easier to stand and watch.
> I could pray a prayer and just move on like nothing's wrong
> But I refuse, 'cause I don't want to live like I don't care
> I don't want to say another empty prayer.
> Oh I refuse to sit around and wait for someone else
> to do what God has called me to do myself.
> Oh, I could choose not to move but I Refuse."

And I refuse to let America be invaded by an unwelcome guest, an illegal alien, an unclean, evil spirit who has tried to denigrate, destroy, and desecrate our spiritual and biblical history in Christ. I stand on the shoulders of many devout and dedicated believers.

George Washington, Benjamin Franklin, Patrick Henry, Daniel Webster, Chief Justice John Marshall, Dwight Eisenhower, George H.W. Bush, George W. Bush, to name a few, are Americans who have stood for righteous living under the divine precepts of God.

Patrick Henry, an eloquent politician stated, "It cannot be emphasized too strongly or too often that this great nation was founded not by religionists but by Christians, not a religion, but on the gospel of Jesus Christ." Henry recognized as did others that we cannot negate or nullify the fact and truth that this is a country founded under the dictates of a living God; our strength was established on the gospel of Jesus Christ.

On the Washington Monument is a sculpture with George Washington kneeling in prayer, on the highest point in the nation's capitol is embedded, in Latin, are the words, "Praise Be Unto God."

Andrew Johnson, this country's 17th president, stated, "Let us look forward to the time when we can take the flag of our country and nail it below the cross, and there let it wave as it waved in the older times, and let us gather around it and inscribed for our motto: 'Liberty and Union, one and inseparable, now and forever,' and exclaim Christ first, our country next."

In his farewell address of September 19, 1796, President George Washington acknowledges the paramount placement and necessity of adherence to faith based on Holy and Biblical jurisdiction to be recognized and lived here in America. He declared, "Of all the dispositions and habits which lead to political prosperity, religion and morality are indispensable supports...and whereas acknowledging the Bible as an integral part of the fabric of our society..."

The evidence mounts….

"On September 11, 1777 the Continental Congress adopted a resolution to import 20,000 Bibles from Holland, and Scotland as the colonies were at war with England…" A day America will remember is, September 11, 2001. The same date but different year that we brought in 20,000 Bibles is the same date that our country was terrorized because of our beliefs in the one, true living Savior. Think about it. We promote God through the living word. We invite life through Jesus Christ with a mass distribution of 20,000 Bibles on September 11, 1777. It is on the same day in 2001 that America, a country which was founded on Biblical principles, is terrorized through an attack by a group who loathes the Name of Jesus as Lord and Savior. Do we see a connection yet?

When the enemy comes in like a flood, God will hold up a standard. The enemy, Satan, seeks to steal, kill, and destroy. He has manipulated and tricked America by loss of sight and vision. Initially America had a vision of Kingdom thinking that God planted in the founding fathers and us to promote Kingdom of God living through acceptance and adherence to these precepts through Jesus Christ. But our vision was clouded by a lack of knowledge of who America really is through Christ. With the influx of contrary thoughts to the word of God such as free thinking as promoted by Greek, Romans, Babylonian, Persian, and other false perspectives, America was stripped of her peace, prosperity, and right standing in God. But lift up your face America, Justice is coming. We are blessed. We are the head and not the tail. We are a chosen generation.

Jesus taught us how to pray. In Matthew Chapter 6: 9 - 13 reads,

"Our Father which art in heaven, Hallowed be thy name. Thy kingdom come. Thy will be done in earth, as it is in heaven. Give us this day our daily bread. And forgive us our debts, as we forgive our debtors. And lead us not into temptation, but deliver us from evil: For thine is the kingdom, and the power, and the glory, forever. Amen."

We must return to God. We must reverse the curse. We are a nation founded under God. We must put prayer back in American Schools.

About the Author

I reside in Southern Ohio with my blessed and courageous twin boys. We actively and boldly proclaim the good news of the Kingdom. To God Be The Glory.